BROAD SHOULDERS
&
TIGHT ENDS

A Football Primer

by Yvonne Ameche
and Jeri Braatz

Dear Joe,
Now that you're
retired, you may
turn into the
guy on page 112.
Much happiness.

Fondly,
Jeri

Enjoy!
Happy to
hear all was
well!
Yvonne

Illustrated by Walt Stewart

Broad Shoulders and Tight Ends
A Football Primer

Co-Authors: Jeri Braatz and Yvonne Ameche

Editor: Catherine Cappelletti

Graphic Design: Maryland Media Associates

Illustrations by Walt Stewart

Printed in the United States of America by Madden Communications Inc., Chicago, Illinois.
TXU 572 152
Summary: An unusual football primer accented with humorous drawings.
ISBN 0-9640964-0-4

For Tom…who not only
wined and dined us,
but also responded patiently
to our continuous questions.
A weaker man would not have endured!

About the Authors

Yvonne Ameche and **Jeri Braatz** have been friends since childhood. Growing up in Kenosha, Wisconsin, they both married their high school sweethearts who had been outstanding players on their championship high school football team.

Alan and Yvonne Ameche moved to Madison, where Alan attended the University of Wisconsin. He started at fullback all four years, starring in the 1954 Rose Bowl and eventually becoming the University's only Heisman Trophy winner. A number one draft choice of the Baltimore Colts, he played on two championship teams. He scored the winning touchdown in the 1958 Championship Game, a game some still refer to as "The Greatest Game Ever Played." Alan enjoyed great success in the business world before his death in 1988. Yvonne now resides in Malvern, Pennsylvania, where she has begun a new career as a public speaker. Yvonne and Alan had six children.

Jeri and Tom Braatz moved to Milwaukee where Tom captained the Marquette University football team before playing for the Dallas Cowboys and Washington Redskins. Since his playing days he has continued to be involved with the National Football League (NFL) as Personnel Director, General Manager, and Vice-President of Football Operations. They raised two sons in Atlanta, Georgia, where Jeri was involved in antiques and the real estate business while Tom was with the Atlanta Falcons. The Braatzes now reside in Miami, Florida, where Tom is the Director of College Scouting for the Miami Dolphins.

While playing for the Dallas Cowboys, Tom and Jeri met **Walt Stewart** who later became a courtroom artist for NBC. Some of his most famous trials include those of Charles Manson, Patty Hearst, and John DeLorean. His illustrations have made him a three-time Emmy award winner. Walt is a native Californian and presently lives north of San Francisco in Marin County.

Though Yvonne, Jeri, and Walt's lives have taken many different directions, they have maintained their long and lasting friendship. This book is their perspective of the football world. Learn and laugh with them!

Table of Contents

III

Football! Oh football! What's in a name?
Are you really a war and we call you a game?

Disciplined troops inhabit your camps,
hidden away from hard liquor and tramps.

On ballfield or battlefield brave generals lead
through cheap shots and pot shots and battle fatigue.

In uniformed lineups, men learn to survive.
The strongest and toughest emerge still alive.

Coaches plot strategies, secretive schemes,
while battlefield action brings choirs of screams.

Competition increases; hostility grows.
Our only objective…to conquer our foes!

Watch for their signals, prepare to reload!
A prize for the man who deciphers their code!

During each conflict, bombs fill the air,
the Blitzkrieg in London might even compare.

For those in the trenches during the game,
the end of the battle spells glory or shame.

Coaches, like generals, demand victory.
Their war games are battles that fans pay to see.

Oh, football! We love your return every season.
Whether war or a game, you will *never* know treason.

Dedication

Prologue

Football is fantasy…it's reality.
It's brutality.
Jubilation…frustration.
Depression…obsession.
Tradition…rivalry.
Passion…aggression.

It's over-achievers and under-achievers.
It's color-coded mania.
Logos…mascots.
Cheers and boos.

It's tailgating and anticipating.
Big biz…show biz.
Fortune…misfortune.
Fame…shame…blame.
Strategy…timing…luck.

It's cohesive and divisive.
Affection and defection.
Sportsmanship…showmanship.
Gamesmanship…championship.

It's millionaires…it's malcontents.
It's celebrities.
Winners and whiners and wannabes.
Losers…guessers…groupies.
But, most of all…
FOOTBALL IS FUN!!!

VI

Chapter I
(We're on the Fifty...)

A Bewildering Puzzle

(She did not read *Broad Shoulders and Tight Ends*.)

She'd never seen a football game but knew it was his passion.
Her date attempted to explain, but then his face grew ashen.

The game was now beginning...no time for idle chatter.
His eyes were fixed upon the field...a life and death matter.

Before they play, a coin is tossed, a ref is out there flipping.
Are they gardening or trimming hair when someone yells, "He's clipping!"

One guy is in a shotgun, then in a pocket, too.
A wave is going through the stands. Can this whole scene be true?

Has the world gone crazy? A wave is in the ocean.
Someone takes a "hand-off!" A back field is in motion?

One player gives a cheap shot. It must be gin or whiskey.
The way they carry on out there, survival must be risky.

An end is tight, receiver...wide, a quarterback is sneaking.
Did they all drink those cheap shots? The crowd is wildly shrieking!

Blitzing! Holding! Splitting out! One guy just made a sack!
At least one thing makes sense out there...a tail *is* in the back.

Their dog is red, their kicker's short, they sweep without a broom.
And when his team scores zero points, her boyfriend's face spells doom.

The announcer doesn't sound alarmed. Next, what will these guys try?
He says that 2 or 3 of them are now in someone's "eye!"

The game was almost over. Did everyone have fun?
A ref went out to warn them. He even took a gun.

This game was too confusing. She had a real strong hunch,
he took the gun out on the field to shoot the whole damn bunch!

The Game

The field is a rectangle measuring 120 yards long and 53 yards wide. Ten yards at each end of the field are designated as "end zones" making the actual playing field 100 yards with "goal lines" at each end. Hashmarks are five yards apart, and in line with the goal posts or uprights which are at each end of the field. The surface is either natural grass or artificial turf.

The Score is achieved by the following means:

A Touchdown —to run or pass the ball over the opponent's goal line for 6 points.

A Conversion—to kick the ball through the goal posts for 1 point or run or pass the ball over the opponent's goal line from the 2-yard line (professional) or 3-yard line (college) for 2 points. A touchdown must be scored before the conversion can be attempted.

A Field Goal—to kick the ball through the uprights from any ball placement within the hash marks for 3 points.

A Safety—to tackle a ball carrier or passer in his own end zone for 2 points or to be charged with an offensive penalty in one's own end zone for 2 points.

The Game begins with the coin toss by the referee. The team that wins the coin toss can elect to receive the ball (offensive team), or kick off and defend their goal (defensive team). Each team defends their half of the field. The object of the game is to pass or run with the ball across the opponents' goal line or kick the ball through the goal posts. Each play begins on the line of scrimmage where the ball is "spotted" by the officials. The offense gets 4 downs (numbered 1st to 4th) to gain 10 yards and make a new 1st down, thus progressing downfield into the scoring zone.

The Time of play is 60 minutes, divided into four 15-minute quarters. However, it normally takes at least 3 hours to complete a game. A tied game results in a 15-minute overtime period in which the first team to score is proclaimed the winner. There is an intermission between halves. Both teams are allowed three 90-second time-outs each half during which the game clock is stopped. Official time-outs may also be called for injuries, measuring yardage, penalties and two-minute warnings which indicate that 2 minutes of playing time remain in each half. There are seven referees officiating the game.

Offensive Team

There are always eleven players on the offensive team, regardless of the formation.

The Down Linemen—line up on the line of scrimmage: two tackles, two guards, and a center.

The Tight End—is normally on the line of scrimmage next to the offensive tackle but is sometimes split out in the slot or placed in motion.

The Wide Receiver—is normally situated on the line of scrimmage and is split out five to ten yards from the offensive tackle or placed in motion.

The Running Back—is normally lined up in the backfield but can be split out as a receiver or placed in motion.

The Quarterback—stands behind the center ready to receive the ball when it is snapped. In the shotgun formation, the quarterback is five to seven yards behind the center.

In the huddle, the quarterback calls the formation, the play, and the snap count, after which he says "break" and the team moves to the line of scrimmage to set up the formation. When the quarterback is in position behind the center, he analyzes the defense to be certain the play called has a reasonable chance to succeed. If not, he calls an audible to change the play at the line of scrimmage to one which he thinks has a better chance of defeating the defensive formation.

College football is predominantly a run-oriented offense. Professional football, on the other hand, is mostly pass-oriented. Therefore, in professional football, you will see multiple offensive formations.

The team that controls the line of scrimmage usually wins!

5

Offensive Formations

Pro Football's Basic Offensive Formations

Offensive Plays

Bootleg
This play appears to be going to one side as the quarterback fakes a handoff. Hiding the ball, he runs around the other end.

Draw Play
To the defense, this looks like a pass, but it is a delayed running play.

Delay
Also called a "check pass," a running back waits for a three-count, then goes over the middle to make a reception.

Reverse
A trick running play. The quarterback fakes toward one direction but hands off to a receiver going in the opposite direction (same as the end around). If that receiver then hands off to another ball carrier moving in the opposite direction, it is called a "double reverse."

Flea Flicker
A fake running play. The quarterback hands the ball to a running back. The back stops short of the line of scrimmage and laterals the ball back to the quarterback, who then throws it downfield for an attempted touchdown.

Hail Mary
A desperation pass at the end of the half or the end of the game, designed with wide receivers congregated in the end zone.

Play-Action
The line blocks as if for a run. The quarterback fakes a run, then passes.

Quarterback Draw
The quarterback drops back to fake a pass and runs the ball up the middle.

Quarterback Sneak
The quarterback takes the snap from the center and immediately runs or dives over the line of scrimmage. A short-yardage play.

End Around

A reverse play in which the wide receiver ends up carrying the ball.

Rollout

A pass play in which the quarterback leaves the pocket and rolls to one side or the other prior to passing the ball.

Run and Shoot

An offensive scheme with the quarterback in the shotgun position using five wide receivers and no tight end or running back.

Screen Pass

The quarterback drops back to pass. The offensive linemen allow pass rushers by, then form a screen of blockers so the ball can be thrown to a running back or receiver behind the screen.

Sweep

A wide running play around the end, usually led by pulling linemen.

Trap

A running play in which a defensive lineman is blocked by a pulling guard, tackle, or tight end behind the line of scrimmage.

Shotgun

The quarterback sets up five to seven yards behind the line of scrimmage to receive the snap from the center. Usually from this position he will pass the ball.

Defensive Team

Astrong defense is one of the most important phases of the game. If your opponent cannot score on you, you will not lose.

Defense takes great athletic ability as defensive players must respond to a series of unknown situations as presented by the offensive team. The defense does not know where they will line up as they must always adjust to the offensive formation. They will be a little behind at the start of every play. They must ignore the fakes of the offense, have a nose for the ball, and stop the play.

They will either hit or get hit, be the "hitter" or the "hittee." The players who are the most aggressive and who hit the hardest will come out on top. A defensive player can measure his value to the team by his distance from the ball at the end of the play.

Down Linemen—normally consists of two tackles and two ends, which is a four-man front, or two ends and a nose tackle, which is a three-man front. They take their positions opposite the offensive linemen.

Inside Linebackers—line up off the line of scrimmage, normally facing a center or an offensive guard.

Outside Linebackers—the linebacker on the strong side normally lines up facing a tight end. The linebacker on the weak side plays off the line of scrimmage. The linebackers key on both offensive linemen and running backs.

The Secondary (Cornerbacks and Safeties)—cornerbacks are the outside defenders who must cover pass receivers all over the field and are supportive against the run. Safeties are inside defenders. The strong safety plays to the side of the tight end while the free safety plays to the side of the split end/wide receiver.

Nickel Defense
A defensive pass formation in which five defensive backs are in the game. The fifth is called the "nickel back."

Dime Defense
A defensive pass formation in which cornerbacks or safeties replace linebackers, allowing for six defensive backs in the coverage.

Prevent Defense
A defensive alignment wherein there is deep zone coverage designed to stop long passes.

Goal Line
A formation used within five yards of the goal line wherein six down linemen set up inside the offensive blockers.

Bump and Run
A technique on pass defense in which the defender jams the receiver as he comes off the line, then sticks with him in man-to-man coverage on his route.

Man-to-Man
A type of pass defense wherein linebackers and defensive backs cover an assigned receiver for the entire play.

Zone Coverage
A type of coverage in which the cornerbacks and safeties are assigned specific areas of the field to cover.

Blitz
A pass rush by a linebacker or a defensive back or both, the purpose of which is to sack the quarterback.

Defensive Plays

11

Officials' Signals

OFFICIAL SIGNALS

Score

Safety

First Down

Time Out

Clock Starts as
Whistle Blows

Delay of Game

Dead Ball or Crowd Noise

Loss of Down

Offside or Encroaching

12

Illegal Contact

Personal Foul

Player Ejected

Ball Illegally Touched,
Kicked, or Batted

Unsportsmanlike Conduct

Illegal Procedure

Holding

Crawling

Intentional
Grounding

Tripping

Illegal Blocking
Below the Waist

13

Illegal Forward Pass

Pass Juggled Inbounds and
Caught Out of Bounds

Invalid Fair Catch

Illegal Motion

Touching a Forward Pass or
Scrimmage Kick

Incomplete Forward Pass
Penalty Refused

Illegal Crackback

Ineligible Receiver Downfield

Pass Interference

X's and O's

Men have an innate ability
to understand X's and O's.
Their minds seem to work with agility
and follow where each player goes.

When the team is lined up at the scrimmage line,
and down in a three-point stance,
a guy can tell in a wink of time
what each player will do at a glance.

They see each player's traps and blocks,
their blitzes, hits, and sacks.
They know which guy is gifted,
or even what he lacks.

Each play details a battle
of strength and great finesse.
A man-fan picks out winners
without a second guess.

But gal-fans are getting more savvy
about talks that go on in the huddle.
They understand the rules and regs
and terms that once were a muddle.

So, gentlemen, think not of ladies
as frivilous bits of frill,
who know not of the end zone
and "bombs" that make you thrill.

The game is becoming co-ed.
It's true without a doubt!
It goes back to that saying,
"Join 'em or be left out!"

15

Helpful Hints
for Football Watchers

Here are some helpful hints which will increase your enjoyment of the game and will help you to understand why a play succeeds or fails.

The player positions listed below wear jerseys that are usually numbered as follows:

Position	Numbers
Quarterbacks	1–19
Running Backs	20–49
Centers	50–59
Guards	60–69
Tackles	70–79
Tight Ends	80–89
Wide Receivers	80–89
Nose Tackles	60–69
Defensive Ends	70–80
Defensive Linemen Can Also Be Numbered	90–99
Linebackers	50–59
Defensive Corners	20–49
Defensive Safeties	20–49

Do not watch the ball. When the ball is snapped, watch the offensive linemen. Their first movement indicates pass or run. If they charge forward across the line of scrimmage, the play will be a run. If they step back, the play will usually be a pass. Watch which way the guards pull and the pattern of the offensive blocking.

Don't forget your binoculars!!!

In the game of football, winning is essential! Fans, critics, owners, and coaches demand victory. A sell-out crowd and a thunderous ovation at the opening kickoff indicate the importance of each regular season game. Each year the race begins anew. The stakes are high!

The events on the field unify a diversified group of people as do few other events in their lives. They cheer together. They wave together. They fall silent together. They are united in their jubilation after a victory. They are united in their dejection after a defeat.

When a team has more losses than wins, there is blame to be placed. Second guessing, armchair quarterbacking, and finger-pointing often abound. Winning is the only thing!

Sportswriters analyze, criticize, reconstruct, compare, correct, and sometimes influence the opinions of the fans. After a sound defeat, the headlines are not a pretty sight. Winning is the only thing!

Who is to blame? The search for blame is divisive. It is frustrating, exasperating, exhausting, unrelenting. The blame must be placed on someone's shoulders. Are those shoulders wearing football pads, coaching shirts, business suits? It is a very complex equation. Winning is the only thing!

Only by winning games can this unpleasant predicament be avoided. Positive outcomes produce jubilant spirits and expectations are then high. The championship is within reach! Winning is the only thing!

"Winning is the Only Thing"

17

The zenith of every football season is the highly anticipated Super Bowl game, in which the two best teams in the country battle it out for the world championship. Every coach dreams of coaching a team in the Super Bowl. Every player dreams of playing in one. Every fan dreams of attending one.

It is the ultimate football contest. Each team in the National Football League plans, practices, prepares, and prays to win this prize. To be the best, the most respected, to end the football season triumphantly wearing the Super Bowl ring, is as good as it gets...and is followed by one joyful, hell-raisin' victory party. Let the champagne flow! To win this one is to be able to say with unparalleled pride, "We are number one!"

"Super Sunday" is a global happening. It is written about, read about, discussed, and debated all over the planet. The host city captures millions of entertainment dollars. The TV sponsors pay premium bucks for brief minutes of advertisements viewed by the entire world. Every aspect of this game is super...the hype, the heraldry, the heroism, the half-time show!

Following the flourish and all the frantic fanfare, disappointment fills the sports lover's world if the game is not competitive. Excitement is what every fan seeks. A clutch game is a thriller...a super high for the viewer! This is the day for every man's personal best. There is no win or loss more glaring than that of Super Sunday. The winner knows elation. The loser knows despair.

Along with all of the preparation and talent, some teams are also kissed by lady luck. They emerge as the victors, the heroes, the dream team! Fame and fortune often follow these fellows for the rest of their lives.

The game lives on...to be discussed and replayed, long after the final seconds of play are history.

Super Bowl

19

Chapter II
(We're on the Forty...)

What Are Your Odds?

Did you know that in the United States

of **265,000** high school seniors who play football,

16,450 make a college team.

This figure dwindles to **8,930** who start as college seniors.

215 make a professional football team.

The odds of a high school football player becoming a professional football player are

1,233 to 1.

Each February, the NFL tests the top college football players with physicals and workouts. These prospects are weighed, measured, and tested for strength, speed, leaping ability, and quickness.

Strength: Number of repetitions a person can do in a bench press position with 225 pounds on the barbell.

Verticle Jump: A standing, upward flat-footed leap to see how high a person can jump.

Leap: A standing broad jump is measured from the starting line to the player's heel.

Short Shuttle: Number of seconds it takes to cover a 20-yard agility drill.

The following are the best, average, and minimum scores in each area tested:

CENTER	BEST	AVERAGE	LEAST
Height	6'6"	6'2"	6'1"
Weight	290 lbs.	280 lbs.	260 lbs.
Strength	29 reps.	22 reps.	16 reps.
40-Yard Dash	5.1 secs.	5.3 secs.	5.6 secs.
Vertical Jump	28"	24"	21"
Leap	9'2"	8'8"	7'7"
Short Shuttle	4.3 secs.	4.5 secs.	4.8 secs.
Arm Length	35"	33"	30"

GUARD			
Height	6'5"	6'3"	6'2"
Weight	335 lbs.	300 lbs.	280 lbs.
Strength	35 reps.	26 reps.	15 reps.
40-Yard Dash	4.9 secs.	5.3 secs.	5.5 secs.
Vertical Jump	30"	26"	15"
Leap	9'8"	8'5"	7'3"
Short Shuttle	4.3 secs.	4.7 secs.	5.0 secs.
Arm Length	35"	33"	32"

23

TACKLE	BEST	AVERAGE	LEAST
Height	6'7"	6'5"	6'3"
Weight	360 lbs.	310 lbs.	280 lbs.
Strength	31 reps.	22 reps.	14 reps.
40-Yard Dash	5.0 secs.	5.4 secs.	5.8 secs.
Vertical Jump	31"	25"	21"
Leap	9'4"	8'3"	7'4"
Short Shuttle	4.4 secs.	4.8 secs.	5.2 secs.
Arm Length	36"	34"	32"

TIGHT END			
Height	6'5"	6'3"	6'0"
Weight	285 lbs.	245 lbs.	220 lbs.
Strength	28 reps.	19 reps.	8 reps.
40-Yard Dash	4.6 secs.	4.9 secs.	5.2 secs.
Vertical Jump	35"	31"	26"
Leap	10'2"	9'4"	8'5"
Short Shuttle	4.2 secs.	4.4 secs.	4.6 secs.
Arm Length	34"	32"	30"

WIDE RECEIVERS			
Height	6'4"	5'11"	5'7"
Weight	235 lbs.	190 lbs.	149 lbs.
40-Yard Dash	4.3 secs.	4.6 secs.	4.9 secs.
Vertical Jump	43"	34"	26"
Leap	10'10"	9'9"	8'7"
Short Shuttle	3.8 secs.	4.2 secs.	4.6 secs.
Arm Length	34"	31"	29"

FULLBACK			
Height	6'2"	6'0"	5'10"
Weight	255 lbs.	235 lbs.	206 lbs.
Strength	27 reps.	17 reps.	11 reps.
40-Yard Dash	4.5 secs.	4.8 secs.	5.0 secs.
Vertical Jump	34"	30"	24"
Leap	9'9"	9'0"	8'6"
Short Shuttle	4.0 secs.	4.4 secs.	4.7 secs.
Arm Length	33"	31"	29"

HALFBACK	BEST	AVERAGE	LEAST
Height	6'2"	5'11"	5'6"
Weight	255 lbs.	200 lbs.	165 lbs.
Strength	22 reps.	14 reps.	5 reps.
40-Yard Dash	4.4 secs.	4.6 secs.	4.9 secs.
Vertical Jump	41"	34"	29"
Leap	11'5"	9'8"	8'7"
Short Shuttle	3.9 secs.	4.2 secs.	4.6 secs.
Arm Length	33"	30"	28"

QUARTERBACK			
Height	6'6"	6'2"	5'11"
Weight	240 lbs.	215 lbs.	190 lbs.
40-Yard Dash	4.6 secs.	4.9 secs.	5.3 secs.
Vertical Jump	36"	30"	23"
Leap	10'2"	8'11"	7'2"
Short Shuttle	4.0 secs.	4.4 secs.	4.8 secs.
Arm Length	34"	31"	29"

DEFENSIVE END			
Height	6'6"	6'3"	6'2"
Weight	292 lbs.	266 lbs.	234 lbs.
Strength	25 reps.	20 reps.	17 reps.
40-Yard Dash	4.7 secs.	4.9 secs.	5.2 secs.
Vertical Jump	33"	31"	28"
Leap	10'3"	9'5"	8'6"
Short Shuttle	4.2 secs.	4.5 secs.	4.9 secs.
Arm Length	35"	33"	31"

DEFENSIVE TACKLE			
Height	6'5"	6'3"	6'1"
Weight	368 lbs.	300 lbs.	267 lbs.
Strength	40 reps.	26 reps.	18 reps.
40-Yard Dash	4.9 secs.	5.1 secs.	5.3 secs.
Vertical Jump	33"	28"	23"
Leap	9'9"	8'10"	8'2"
Short Shuttle	4.1 secs.	4.5 secs.	4.8 secs.
Arm Length	34"	32"	31"

25

DEFENSIVE CORNER	BEST	AVERAGE	LEAST
Height	6'3"	5'10"	5'7"
Weight	210 lbs.	187 lbs.	164 lbs.
Strength	20 reps.	12 reps.	2 reps.
40-Yard Dash	4.4 secs.	4.6 secs.	4.7 secs.
Vertical Jump	43"	36"	29"
Leap	11'3"	10'1"	9'
Short Shuttle	3.9 secs.	4.2 secs.	4.5 secs.
Arm Length	34"	32"	30"

FREE SAFETY			
Height	6'3"	6'1"	5'9"
Weight	218 lbs.	203 lbs.	180 lbs.
Strength	19 reps.	12 reps.	10 reps.
40-Yard Dash	4.4 secs.	4.6 secs.	4.8 secs.
Vertical Jump	38"	34"	30"
Leap	10'6"	9'1"	9'
Short Shuttle	4.0 secs.	4.2 secs.	4.5 secs.
Arm Length	34"	31"	29"

STRONG SAFETY			
Height	6'3"	6'0"	5'9"
Weight	224 lbs.	206 lbs.	195 lbs.
Strength	17 reps.	13 reps.	7 reps.
40-Yard Dash	4.5 secs.	4.7 secs.	4.8 secs.
Vertical Jump	34"	33"	32"
Leap	10'2"	9'7"	8'10"
Short Shuttle	4.0 secs.	4.2 secs.	4.4 secs.
Arm Length	33"	31"	30"

OUTSIDE LINEBACKER	BEST	AVERAGE	LEAST
Height	6'5"	6'2"	5'11"
Weight	268 lbs.	236 lbs.	221 lbs.
Strength	29 reps.	19 reps.	9 reps.
40-Yard Dash	4.4 secs.	4.8 secs.	5.1 secs.
Vertical Jump	39"	34"	29"
Leap	10'9"	9'8"	8'9"
Short Shuttle	3.9 secs.	4.3 secs.	4.6 secs.
Arm Length	35"	33"	31"

INSIDE LINEBACKER			
Height	6'3"	6'1"	5'11"
Weight	251 lbs.	234 lbs.	215 lbs.
Strength	26 reps.	20 reps.	10 reps.
40-Yard Dash	4.5 secs.	4.8 secs.	5.0 secs.
Vertical Jump	39"	32"	27"
Leap	10'6"	9'4"	8'6"
Short Shuttle	4.0 secs.	4.2 secs.	4.4 secs.
Arm Length	34"	32"	30"

27

Training Camp

The football player's body is the tool of his trade. He works out strenuously off-season to stay in shape. Training camp is a time of pain, pressure, preparation, and puddles of sweat as it becomes his proving ground. He will train his body to be on full alert and will push himself beyond his limits in the weight room and on the field doing conditioning drills—sit-ups, push-ups, grass drills (run in place and hit the dirt), and gassers (sideline to sideline sprints against the clock). His body will turn to steel and he will walk the fine line between perfect muscles and pulled muscles.

The first arrivals are the hopeful rookies, full of fire, enthusiasm, and excitement. This is a dream fulfilled for them...a chance to become a pro. They thrill at the opportunity to meet the vets, the established stars, who were headliners when these rookies were kids. When the scarred and weathered veterans enter camp a few days later, it is during the most brutally hot days of summer.

These are hell weeks. There are two practices a day, often in full pads. They will toil and sweat and ache. They will shout and curse and grumble and mumble unrepeatable expletives. Fast friendships form and friends compete against friends. The rookies may be third or fourth team with a slim chance to make a roster, but they must never become discouraged or give up. They learn mental and physical toughness and play hurt. This lesson in perseverance will serve them well all the days of their lives—never quit!

They consume eighteen-wheelers of food. After practice, comradery and beers are relished as they replace gallons of liquid they lost on the field. During dinner, the rookie show provides lots of laughs as the young guys sing, tell jokes, and do impersonations of their coaches. A few practical jokers will hide and torment the coach who does bed checks at eleven. Some of the more daring may even sneak out of camp. This is risky business.

Not all players will survive. Some are sent to "the Turk" who gives them the grim news that they are "cut" from the team. This unpopular fellow yanks their playbook from their hands and arranges the cheapest one-way ticket home. When they leave this place, they will have thicker necks and thinner waistlines. The survivors will feel the pride of having met and endured one of the most strenuous and grueling challenges of their lives...and the money ain't bad either.

29

QUARTERBACK

H e leads the offense. He calls the signals and the plays. He can either pass, hand off, or run with the ball.

The quarterback is the team's main man,

who calls the plays if coach says he can.

His attributes could be legendary,

if he can pass the ball or sneak and carry.

He must have arm strength and ball handling ability,

be able to scramble and run with agility,

be mentally tough, a competitive leader,

a feisty, decisive, defensive reader.

He's surrounded by linemen who keep him from harm

by protecting their leader and his golden arm.

Quarterback Skills

- Quickness to set up to pass
- Anticipates where receivers will be
- Quick release of ball
- Throws on the run
- Able to take a hit

- Accuracy on both short and long passes
- Communicates and works well with others
- Makes quick decisions
- Is smart and wins

31

RUNNING BACK

These players are designated as "halfbacks" or "tailbacks." They are the main ball carriers in the ground game. They block for each other and also act as receivers.

A breakaway runner with fast swivel hips,

he dodges and fakes as quickly he zips.

Past his defenders, he scampers and scurries,

a darter in here can eliminate worries.

Running Back Skills

- Catlike balance to stay on his feet
- Speed to outrun the defense
- Ability to change direction without losing speed
- Size and willingness to block
- Soft hands and flexibility to adjust to a pass
- Instincts and good peripheral vision to avoid tacklers
- Darting moves to make 'em miss
- Determination not to fumble
- Leg strength to break tackles
- Leaping ability to go over the pile-up

33

This back is responsible for gaining tough, short yardage. He also blocks to create holes for the other running backs.

Fullback

A nose for the goal line with power and speed,

the fullback bursts through for the yardage they need.

Dependable, reliable, a good man in a pinch,

he'll bully his way ahead for every needed inch.

At a goal line stand with fans on their feet,

the coach calls on him to take off the heat!

Fullback Skills

- Possesses a combination of strength and power
- Toughness to block like a guard
- Uncanny ability to read defense
- Ability to find a hole and accelerate
- Durability to carry 20 times a game
- Agility to make tacklers miss
- Ability to run low with shoulders over his knees to break tackles
- Speed to outrun a linebacker
- Determination not to fumble

35

CENTER

The man in the middle of the offensive line. He is responsible for snapping the ball to the quarterback, punter, or placekick holder. He can have one of the longest careers on the team.

Center

The squatting steady center is a man of little fame.

A wild snap over the punter's head, and he will get the blame.

The ball's in his possession at the start of every play.

And then it's his assignment to snap the ball away.

His timing must be perfect, not too soon and not too late.

Accurate snaps to quarterbacks make longevity his fate.

Center Skills

- Snaps the ball to quarterback
- Snaps the ball to punters and kickers
- Balance, power and strength
- Hand and foot speed
- Explosiveness and quickness

37

There are two guards who line up on either side of the center in the offensive line. A guard will often pull to lead the blocking on runs.

The chief assignment of the guards

is to open holes to make those yards.

Nifty feet and body balance

are among his many talents.

With a nasty sneer, he has control

to clear a path, a hefty hole.

With keen instincts, he prevents a sack

by protecting his sacred quarterback.

He's grubby and gritty, a big tough dude,

who couldn't care less if he gets booed!!!

Guard Skills

- Size and strength
- Balance and quickness
- Power and explosiveness
- Ability to knock the opponent off the line of scrimmage
- Tough, smart, and competitive

39

There are two tackles positioned outside of the guards on offense. The left tackle is normally higher paid because he protects a right-handed quarterback's blindside and faces the opponent's best pass rusher.

Tackle

He's big, explosive, strong, and mean,

the tackle is a tough machine.

Onrushing defenders he grabs and shakes

and crushes into flat pancakes.

He loves to batter, bruise, and maul,

and make that defense cry and crawl!!!

Tackle Skills

- Size and strength
- Balance and quickness
- Power and explosiveness
- Tough, smart, and competitive
- Has more finesse than a guard

41

The placement of the tight end determines the strong side of the offensive line.

A receiving end, a blocking end,

this guy is no defender's friend.

Over the middle...a snatched quick pass,

leaving defenders scattered in grass.

He's stout, he's strong...no way a smurf,

a threat on grass or astroturf!

Tight End

Tight End Skills

- Pass catching skills of a wide receiver
- Run blocking tenacity of offensive tackle
- Running ability of a back after making the catch
- Size and strength to knock linebackers backwards
- Speed to "split the seam" and catch the ball deep
- Physical ability to outmuscle defensive backs for the ball
- Quickness to escape the linebacker and make sharp pass cuts

43

WIDE
RECEIVER

Wide Receiver

A pass receiver who lines up outside of the offensive tackle. There may be anywhere from one to four wide receivers on any given play.

His cuts must be sharp! No split second to tarry,

his blurring feet race to collect a "Hail Mary!"

His height is an asset, plus quickness and grace,

he gets open deep with his hands right in place.

Catching a long ball without any sweat,

he gets down the field and is always a threat!

Wide Receiver Skills

- Hands that are soft and supple to catch the ball
- Speed to burst by defensive backs
- Quickness and foot speed to make sharp cuts
- Ability to adjust to ball in the air
- Strength and toughness and willingness to block
- Ability to run and dart after the catch
- Ability to run precise pass patterns
- Ability to absorb the hard hits of the defensive backs

45

NOSE TACKLE

Nose Tackle

The defensive tackle in a 3-4 alignment who lines up in the middle of the line opposite the center.

Tank-like and quick with a nose for the ball,

this bulldozing mauler can cover it all.

The pass or the run can both make him grin,

he loves wiping offensive guys off his chin.

Nose Tackle Skills

- Quickness on the snap of the ball
- Hand and arm strength to throw the center
- Size and power to fill the hole over the center
- Speed with range to catch the ball carrier
- Steady surge to flush the quarterback
- Aggressiveness to make plays

47

KOSKOLKOWSKI'S 15th SACK

Wide set defensive lineman usually set opposite offensive tackles, responsible for rushing the passer and stopping the run.

"Sack, sack the quarterback!"

is the chant that comes from the stands.

The defensive end is hungry

for that quarterback's bones in his hands.

Behind the line of scrimmage,

the play is getting set.

This end is thinking, "mincemeat,"

and then makes good his threat !!!

Defensive End Skills

- Quickness and speed off the ball
- Hand and arm strength to jerk offensive lineman off balance
- Size to anchor in the hole to stop the run
- Tenacity to make big plays and tackle ball carriers
- Durability to be there for every game

Defensive End

49

LINEBACKER

Linebacker

The defender who plays between defensive linemen and defensive backs. In 3-4 alignments, linebackers are designated "inside" and "outside." In 4-3 alignments, they are designated "outside" and "middle."

Those vicious tenacious linebacker's eyes,

are ever alert for the offensive guys.

They think they can juke him out of his shoes,

they won't quickly forget the pain that ensues!

Linebacker Skills

- Reads and reacts on the snap of the ball
- Protects his body from blockers with strong hands and arms
- Rugged tackler who's tough and aggressive
- Strength to hold his ground when the run is at him
- Athletic ability of a basketball player to cover pass
- Speed to chase and catch the ball carrier
- An instinctive nose for the ball

51

CORNERBACK

52

A player in the defensive secondary. He is set wide to the side of the formation and is responsible for pass coverage and stopping running plays.

He watches the ball and must quickly assess

a run or a pass...not be fooled by finesse.

If the ball's in the air and is headed downfield,

he must stay man-to-man and can't ever yield.

To the receiver he must allow clearance,

or hear the dread call by the ref, "Interference!"

Cornerback Skills

- Fine athletic skills like a basketball player
- Body and foot control to stop and start on a dime
- Goes for the interception instead of making tackles
- Smarts to decipher the pass from the run fake

- Ruggedness to tackle the ball carrier
- Aggressiveness to challenge the receiver
- Speed to break on to the ball in the air

53

Defensive Safety

Safeties line up as the two deepest defenders inside of the cornerbacks in the defensive formation. The "strong" safety is responsible for covering the tight end. The "free" or "weak" safety lines up on the side away from the tight end and plays the deepest of the defensive backs.

This defensive guy is wiley and speedy,

he covets the balls with eyes quick and greedy.

He back-pedals toward a receiver so tall,

hoping and praying for a piece of that ball!!!

Defensive Safety Skills

- Has smarts to read the run or the pass quickly
- Tough and aggressive to force the run
- Speed and range to go get the ball
- Leadership to make the vocal calls
- Shoulder and arm strength to ward off blocks
- Soft hands to intercept

55

KICKER

Placekicker

The player who kicks off to start the game and the second half. He also kicks field goals and extra points from a fixed point where the ball has been placed by a holder.

The crowd's on their feet, the sidelines are frantic!

The kicker's called in, his eyes display panic!

The score's 10 to 10, with a minute to play,

if he makes the kick, he's the hero today.

But if he should shank it...his heart's in his throat,

his teammates avoid him and now he's the goat!!!

Placekicker Skills

- Precise steps and approach to the ball
- Accuracy
- Leg strength
- Kickoff hang time and range
- Can handle pressure situations
- Infrequently he will fake the kick and will pass or run

57

PUNTER

Punter

The player who punts the ball normally on fourth down, resulting in a change of possession. His "hang-time" is of utmost importance as he strives to hit the "coffin corner."

When it's fourth down and they're in a hole,

he'll boom that ball toward the other goal.

He hopes his hang-time is long enough,

so the suicide squad can do their stuff.

Tensions mount as thousands roar!

Don't let that opposing return man score!

Punter Skills

- Precise steps to deliver punt
- Technique and consistency
- Leg strength and hang-time
- Accuracy to coffin corner
- Soft hands to catch snap

59

Chapter III
(We're on the Thirty...)

A football team for sale today is worth a pricey buck.
The owner who bought years ago had quite a piece of luck.

His wise investment has been great in net appreciation,
since football now is truly an obsession in our nation.

He hires, fires, names, and blames...headmaster of his school.
The man who has the hard cold cash, it's he who makes the rule.

His limo pulls up to the game and lets the owner out,
his golden rule is in effect, he has enormous clout!

His luxury box awaits him, and from this lofty view,
he happily anticipates a pile of revenue!

Owner

63

He's a man with a mission...to win a Super Bowl!
On offense and on defense, his team must take control.

From his personnel director to the water boy,
all must strive together to achieve a common joy.

His scouting staffs get schedules, go out and hit the road,
position by position, they grade the player load.

Picks and trades are critical to upgrade a struggling team,
then, signing guys, it's no surprise, is not a GM's dream.

Haggling with the agents, there still is quite a gap.
Everybody wants their share within the salary cap.

His head coach pick, without a doubt, is his main decision,
if he's right, the team has might, avoiding fans' derision.

If all things are propitious, and the football gods smile down,
the general manager could be the happiest guy in town!

General Manager

65

Head Coach

The head coach is the king pin, the honored chief of state.
His decisions are all major if a win he'll orchestrate.

The game plans are his doing, so a brilliant football mind
will keep the fans from booing. His team won't lag behind.

His judgement must be faultless in his coaching staff selection.
Each coach has his assignments and strives to reach perfection.

An innovator, a motivator, a man with great aplomb,
whose head won't swell from victories and, in defeat, stays calm.

He's in a bold position for the credit or the blame.
He lives and dies with all his guys in each and every game.

No failure is accepted for any type of reason.
The win-loss column seals his fate at the end of every season.

He may go out on shoulders in a blaze of winning glory,
or get those walking papers. Too frequently the story!

67

HEAD COACH (LOSING)

Armchair Coach

"You should have done it this way." But if the coach had done it,
they'd surely say that way was wrong, even if he'd won it.

They second-guess the referee, the draft, the coach, the calls.
How brilliant are these gentlemen, these wondrous know-it-alls!

What they didn't know on Saturday, they always know on Sunday.
And overnight, they all turn bright, they're geniuses on Monday.

Whether the down be 3rd and short, or if it's 4th and long,
they're going to know exactly why that call had gone so wrong.

The second-guesser's team would be such awesome sheer perfection,
his quarterback could take a nap behind his staunch protection.

Every down would be a 1st, the ball they'd never yield.
There would be no mistakes, a perfect team they'd field.

The kicker on this magic team would have a magic toe.
The football that departs his foot would know just where to go.

The center snaps just right each time and masters long snaps, too.
His blocking stops them on a dime, just tell him what to do.

The QB never misses, with finesse that's oh, so fine.
His bootlegs and his handoffs would fool them every time!

The game plan is, of course, each week the absolute solution.
Offense, defense, to a man, give perfect execution.

No druggies, droppers, hot-heads here, no illegal formations.
Their awesome execution always causes wild sensations.

The lightning-like receiver, with those amazing sticky hands,
goes down the field so quickly, a roar goes through the stands.

With armchair champs as coaches, we'd be on a roll.
With armchair champs as coaches, we'd win the Super Bowl!

69

A coaching staff is a group of guys
who teach techniques and specialize.

Dispensing playbooks to their men,
they repeat each detail again and again.

It's a red-eye job creating winners,
that finds them facing midnight dinners.

When a head coach leaves, his staff, it seems,
must also join with other teams.

For those who shine, they get their thanks,
when asked to join head coaching ranks.

Assistant Coach

71

A scout's life is travel for he's always on the road.
He sees each college prospect in an analyzing mode.

His days are in film rooms, on fields, or on flights.
Then writing reports consumes all of his nights.

He stalks college campuses seeking a "sleeper,"
a player who's gifted in all ways a "keeper."

His tools are a stopwatch and a tape measure,
he's ready to rate every potential treasure.

His judicious judgements are surely not rash,
as he times prospects in the forty-yard dash.

Looking for quickness, speed, and agility,
he tests for strength and leaping ability.

College trainers tell him which players are hurt,
college coaches tell him which ones are alert.

Which guy is bright, which guy is mean,
which one does drugs, which one is clean.

Does a player have promise to line up and start?
Some talents are evident, but what's in his heart?

Scout

73

PUBLIC RELATIONS DIRECTOR

74

From the Super Bowl to an everyday scrimmage,
the PR Department must shine the team image.

Press updates are released when the players are signed,
presenting goody-two-shoes, so no one is maligned.

No DUIs, druggies, nor robbers who loot,
and oh please, don't mention "paternity suit!"

No brawlers or maulers who make the headlines.
Each player is wearing a halo that shines.

If the highlight film has nothing to please,
the PR man, too, may be caught catching zzzzzzzzzz's.

If the season is lousy and morale very low,
this guy can still make the scenario glow.

When the press arrives, there's a smile on his face,
as he vows that his team will explode to first place.

Public Relations

75

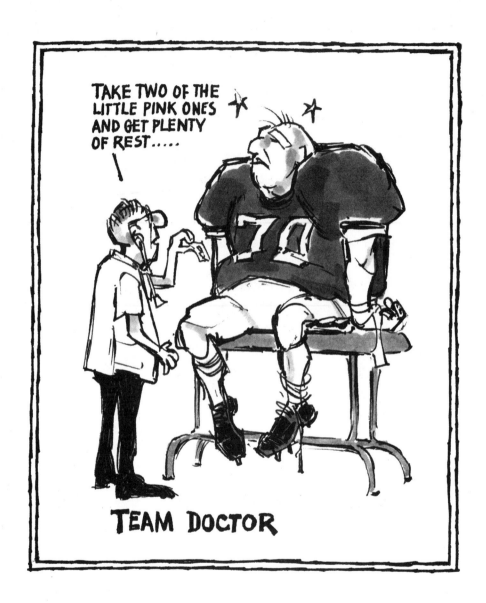

Team Doctor

A broken bone, a torn-up knee,
the team doc is the man to see.

He sutures and prescribes their pills,
diagnosing injuries and ills.

He marches the sidelines alert for the cry,
"Doctor! Doctor! Where the hell is that guy?"

He tends to all their sprains and bumps and bruises.
God only knows how much novocaine he uses!

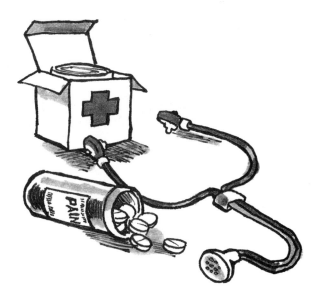

77

The team trainer is the guy who knows the players well.
He treats their wounded bodies as painful injuries swell.

He knows the team's "crybabies" and those who play with pain.
He can tell by instinct if they're ready for a game.

When scouts seek out their prospects for insight and inspection,
a trainer's word is mighty in swaying their selection.

Ankles, wrists, and knees are taped in preparation.
Each player's trust is with him in complete cooperation.

A trainer is a doctor and a mother and a wife.
He helps the guys o'er all the humps involved in football life!

Trainer

79

When the team plays away, and the charter touches down,
this guy is in a scramble to get out on the ground.

A truckload of equipment is his responsibility,
to transport from the home field to opponents' field facility.

Pads, jerseys, helmets, straps, cleats, and socks
are stacked in every locker, ready for the jocks.

At practice or at training camp or in a season game,
his diligence in maintenance is steadfastly the same.

He handles all their discards with their blood, sweat, and tears.
He grieves when they hear boos and thrills when they hear cheers.

Equipment Manager

81

Seven officials in charge of the game
determine infractions and who is to blame.

With fourteen trained eyes, they watch for it all.
They study the football field, players and ball.

Was that pass complete? Did his knee touch the ground?
Was it clipping or tripping? Each call is profound!

The players get nasty and holler and swear.
Irate, drunken fans even throw underwear!

One more yellow flag and the fans hit their feet!
By this Sunday's sundown, that ref is dead meat.

When those flags emerge from a referee's pocket,
blood pressure shoots up like a Carnival rocket.

When coaches insist players' blocks are not clips,
let's hope that the kiddies cannot read their lips!

Referee

83

Chapter IV
(We're on the Twenty...)

The Agent

In the early days of pro football,
there were no agents hot to call.

Players signed contracts and would quickly agree,
then say to themselves, "I'm just happy it's me!"

When training camp starts now, not every guy's there.
Some football fans feel that it just isn't fair.

Those guys don't show up until camp cuts off,
while teammates are sweating their tired butts off.

The agent says money is what it's about
and counsels his client to "keep holding out."

The season kicks off on a Sunday that's sunny.
The agent is missing cause he's counting his money!

87

With knockout good looks and a figure to boot,
not much is covering her birthday suit.

The skirt may be short, the sweater too tight,
but men in the stands think she looks oh, so right!

She wiggles and shakes as she leads them in cheers,
while the guys in the stands leer over their beers.

If women were players, would men bare their all
to support and cheer ladies as they ran the ball?

Cheerleaders

89

The Media

Sports fans want updates everyday
on what the media has to say.

"Who was injured, released, or signed?"
"Who missed bed check and was fined?"

Those daily deadlines must be met
with news and views of rook and vet.

Some analyze. Some criticize.
Some are buddies with the guys.

Eyes light up and smile lines crease
when there's a special press release.

In a post-game conference, they're in a hurry
to surround the coach so they can scurry

to disseminate late information
to anxious fans throughout the nation!

91

Chapter V (The Fans)
(We're on the Ten...)

Barstool Bob

Here they come! The regulars at Shortie's *I'm Not Here* saloon are ready for action!

Bob is the head honcho who holds court from his barstool. He selects the game of the day and enjoys mighty fine dining on pretzels and hard-boiled eggs, as well as Shortie's chili and beans.

The topic is always football and who will win the next game. There's back slappin', knee slappin', and butt slappin'. They have their own mugs, their own stools, and their own football pools.

On game day, Shortie proudly prepares his specialties, Mad-Dog Chili and Run-for-the-Border Beans. Shortie's chili can cause more pain than the meanest man on the football field.

The bartender, Linus Scrimmage, prepares special drinks in honor of the day's opponents with names that cannot be repeated in the presence of ladies. Bob and his buddies order another chilled pitcher of beer and hoot and holler!

Since the sultry barmaid, Bo Dacious, announced that she has a weakness for ballplayers, some of the guys wear football jerseys hoping that their team won't be the only one to score. Bo complains that they should be called for "illegal use of hands" or "unsportsmanlike conduct."

From tailgaters to skyboxers, no fans enjoy the game more than this gang of gladiators…legends in their own minds.

95

Big Bronco
The Old Pro

With creaking joints, gnarled fingers, and scarred knees, the Old Pro has more say and savvy than any other fan. Holding court, surrounded by fans who "knew him when," he answers questions about the good old days. His mind is a databank of details of past games and past names, past plays and glory days. His broken nose forms an "S" curve on the highway of a face that has seen multiple pileups. His "gap eight" has been repaired by modern dental work.

In the early days, the league and the rosters were smaller, so the talent was undiluted. Sixty-minute men played both offense and defense without facemasks. There were no agents or signing bonuses; just a group of "smash-mouth" men who played a beloved game with reckless abandon and audacity. They could be teddy bears at home, but after the coin toss, they became hostile aggressors on the prowl for victory and victims.

Perhaps he lives in the past too much, with laurels that are frayed and worn. Plagued by old injuries, his philosophy is still, "Play hurt. No wimps allowed!" He walked away from many hits that would have put a lesser man in intensive care. The players today may be bigger, stronger, and are definitely richer. But to the Old Pro and his fans, they will never be tougher than those granite gridders...the "old-fashioned sixty-minute men!"

97

Fake Jake
The Phantom Jock

Don't scramble to dig out your old game-day programs. His name was never on an active roster nor any veterans' list. He may have passed through training camp, but he was in and out in a heartbeat.

This wannabe has actually kidded himself into believing he was Mr. All-Pro! He tells tall tales of dazzling runs, spectacular catches, and vicious tackles from a three-point stance and actually limps off after telling them. Most folks are too polite to break his football fantasy bubble.

His conversations are peppered with the names of famous buddies he "played" with or against on fields of battle. His logo-covered clothes are from awards banquets. His jersey number was retired in his honor. "Football is my life," says he, the master of myth.

"Hey Jake! Get a life!"

99

The quintessential optimist, Harry never wants to read, say, or hear anything negative about his team.

Finding the highlights, not the lowlights, is his seasonal search. Naysayers do not influence his unquenchable zeal. Twenty incomplete passes are forgotten in the light of one reception.

This loyal fan enjoys his team, win or lose, with never a "Bah Humbug!" He unhesitatingly renews his season tickets. He displays banners at every game, saves every program, and would wait for a team charter till half-past March. Players, coaches, and management all know him. They love his attitude. Oh, for a stadium full of Harrys!

In his will, he has specified that his cremated remains are to be strewn over the practice field.

He is loyal to the end...and beyond!

Hang-In-There Harry

Someone hid his bullhorn. Not that he needs one. He seems, by some marvel of the mind-body connection, to have developed a "megaphone" voice.

Starved for attention, he paints his face in team colors, dresses as a viking, an Indian chief, or a cave man. Every game day, it's a new rig—from cross-dressing to wearing only a wooden barrel risking slivers in low places.

He is the focal point of his stadium section, frantically cheering and waving. When his team scores, he jumps up and down faster than a newly announced game show contestant.

The crowd quickly becomes bored with his antics. Their amusement turns to annoyance. Their cheers are replaced with catcalls... "Down in front!"..."Bag it, pea brain!"..."Pipe down, pissant!"

Someone once said, "Hey, didn't I see you on TV?" That did it! Now there ain't no stopping Charlie or his best buddy, Bear B. Hinds (the mooner).

Look-Here-And-Cheer Charlie

103

Otto Outburst

Otto is a volcano ready to blow! Get out those blood pressure pills! Don't tell *him* that it's only a game.

When his team is behind, he borders on paranoia. Every penalty, incomplete pass, or turnover is part of some almighty plot to bring him misery.

His wife hides out at the mall. The kids run to the movies. His dog takes a submissive "paws up" posture. He kicks and abuses the TV set. His TV repairman, Holden Cheat, is never the loneliest man in town!

Otto's rage makes him a solitary figure on game day. No one wants to be near this bellowing bully. He's as unwelcome at game day parties as a truckload of Twinkies at a Weight Watchers' meeting.

105

Rita Roundheel
The Pretender

Using feminine wiles, some women will go to great lengths to capture and marry a handsome honey. No one goes to greater lengths and pretenses than Rita Roundheel.

Wanting him to think that she likes what he likes, she agrees to attend a game. She wears her most seductive outfit, and clings to him with breathless, baby-voiced adoration. Her knowledge of football is nil, but she loves the terminology. She always approves a "pass" aimed in her direction and yearns to be "caught in the grasp" or "brought down" on the field. Holding and illegal use of hands are her favorite penalties.

Once they climb to their seats in the last row, the rain begins to fall. Her make-up runs, her hose runs, her nose runs. Into the fourth quarter, it suddenly occurs to her that the only sweet nothing her beloved has whispered in her ear since they have been seated is, "Wanna beer?"

107

Round-A-Down Don

There is always the fan who does not know his limits when he gets his head in a jug of his favorite adult beverage. The more he drinks, the more he weaves to the restroom. Meet Round-A-Down Don.

His slurring commentary grows in volume with each beer. Quarter by quarter, Don becomes increasingly unsteady on his feet. He works his way out of his seat, tripping on toes while sipping on beers and blocking out views. He is as popular as a chain-smoker at a health spa.

His friends, Willy Ketchum, Triptan Fell, and Justin Bounds hope to lose Don in the post-game crowd so that they won't be nagged to stop at the Stagger Inn, his favorite watering hole.

The "morning after," Don claims that he was "over-served." His buddies always have a designated driver. It is *never* Don!

An armchair quarterback, Gus is a chronic malcontent with the disposition of a starving pit bull.

He organizes himself in front of his TV set with his rosters and records and takes detailed notes during every game. These memos make him an instant authority on football strategy.

At the opening kickoff, his mouth goes into a hurry-up-offense. "Wrong play! Trade him! Cut him! Cane him! Fire the coach! Sell the team!" An all-star performance couldn't please him. There's always a way that he could have done it better.

His co-workers, Miss A. Tackle and Miss A. Block, dread the Monday morning rehashing from this smarty pants. His knowledgeable bravado dissolves when they tell him to take his stats and shove 'em.

Second-Guess Gus

111

Spud McDudd

A football fanatic and a TV addict, Spud is arguably the world's most accomplished couch potato. Though he admires the iron-firm forms of his halfback heroes, his own flab flourishes. His resolutions to "shape up" are etched in oatmeal as he organizes his "Sideline Smokers" support group.

When the TV set is on, he moves less than any ambulatory member of the human race. With the first kickoff of the football season, his family bids him farewell. Only his bladder's demands can force him to remove himself from the sofa. Otherwise, he is planted and rooted.

Empty cans, wrappers, bottles, and butts mound around him. He has absolutely no team allegiance. His loyalties lie in a stocked refrigerator and a packed pantry, and his flabby form lies in a landfill.

Even the offensive line couldn't move this guy!

TAILGATE TILLIE

114

Tailgate Tillie

Tailgaters diversify their menus from hot dogs to Beef Wellington; from elegant catered cuisine to liquid lunches.

No one tries to impress her guests as does Tillie. Transporting her equipment is as monumental as transporting the team and their gear.

Linens, candles, flowers, china, and silver service are attended to by her tuxedo-attired servers, Seymour Fortunes and Price C. Seetz. The caterer, Furston Goal, slices, dices, whips, flips, and flames with a flourish. Is Tillie expecting the president?

Tailgaters share a common bond of food, fun, and football fever. But no matter who wins on the field, Tillie's tailgate always triumphs!

115

Undaunted Dan
The All-Weather Fan

Domed stadiums are a boon to most fans who would otherwise pass up a kickoff in inclement weather. Dome or not, the all-weather fan remains undaunted by the weatherman's ominous predictions.

Heat waves or blizzards are never factors in his schedule. His weekend plans remain unaltered. In a heat wave, he strips off his shirt and sits bare-chested. In a blizzard, a sleeping bag becomes his cocoon. In a downpour, he totes ponchos that shelter a hip flask to supply inner warmth. All of his regalia bears team colors and logos, so there's never any question of his allegiance.

His wife reveals that Undaunted Dan becomes Delicate Dan when it comes to weathering the elements to shovel snow or mow the lawn.

Though his team sinks to the cellar, he remains steadfast in his loyalty. His motto, "Just wait till next year!" is uttered through chattering blue lips in December. His sentiments are echoed by his best friends, Victor E. Bowls, Yul B. Winners, and Wade Ago.

Voluptuous Vonnie
The Camp Follower

Around for as long as "the oldest profession known to man," are the camp followers.

Perhaps they waited outside of The Coliseum for their gladiator dates. If the lions won...the wait was a long one.

Football players have been "blessed" with more than their share of these jock chasers. Following teams, this trollop will go to any length to snare her "ticket to the good life."

To see one is to know her...hair perfectly done, cleavage on display, skirt slit to her waist...sexy and seductive. Throwing more come-hither looks than a quarterback throws passes, she is often found outside of the stadium with her girlfriends, Merrie Winner and Tess T. Loozer. They gather and gawk at the guys in the hotel lobby, on the team bus, or peek through locker room doors. They can smell testosterone.

Motivated by a desire for he-man muscle, money, and fame, she is not discouraged by guards or wedding rings.

As we watch her, we can only guess what she does best.

Wally Wager
The Bookie's Buddy

Wally is a compulsive gambler. "Wanna bet?" is his "Have a nice day." Football season is Wally Wager heaven... mention not that betting is against the law. He boasts that lady luck loves him. All week, he ponders his picks and perpetually predicts scores.

He brags that his approach to betting is "scientific" and not merely left to chance. He is the odds expert. If the local team is ahead and the point spread is putting Wally in the loss column, he begins to cheer for the opposition. This really riles his buddies who back the home team. He becomes about as popular as *Heidi* pre-empting a playoff game.

Wally always claims that he "just made a killing." Oh yeah? Then how come his bookie, Fred Spread, drives a baby blue Bentley?

Chapter VI
(Touchdown!)

Up in the Air Over Football

In a recent season, NFL teams flew many miles traveling to preseason and regular season games.

San Francisco Forty-Niners	40,606
Houston Oilers	35,406
Miami Dolphins	33,598
Dallas Cowboys	31,828
Denver Broncos	31,152
Washington Redskins	31,126
Seattle Seahawks	29,470
Los Angeles Rams	29,450
Phoenix Cardinals	27,980
Tampa Bay Buccaneers	25,688
Los Angeles Raiders	25,124
New Orleans Saints	23,408
Buffalo Bills	23,102
Philadelphia Eagles	23,032
New York Giants	22,844
San Diego Chargers	22,092
New England Patriots	21,074
Kansas City Chiefs	17,792
New York Jets	17,262
Atlanta Falcons	16,274
Minnesota Vikings	15,732
Cincinnati Bengals	14,852
Chicago Bears	13,568
Pittsburgh Steelers	13,398
Indianapolis Colts	13,064
Cleveland Browns	12,738
Green Bay Packers	12,354
Detroit Lions	10,688
Total	**634,702**

Source: *USA Today*

124

A mascot is defined as a person, thing, or animal that is supposed to bring good luck. A logo is a trademark. How mascots, logos, and team colors are selected by professional football teams is something of a mystery. Sometimes there is a regional or historic connection, or the selection simply can give the team name a rhythmic ring.

In professional football, there are a great variety of logos and mascots: smiling fish, woolly bison, western dudes, high-flying birds, and ponies. There are ferocious felines, wildcatters, pirates, ursine mammals, Norsemen, Indians, miners, western steeds, sheep, loyalists, goliaths, meat processors, a color—even some holy people. Others have the same names as bolts of lightening and modern aircraft.

All of these trademarks and mascots are represented by their team colors and adorn everything from baby bottles to blankets, from dinnerware to doggy bowls, from underwear to outerwear. Wherever there is a fan, you will likely find evidence of his or her favorite team.

There are thirty professional football teams referred to above. Can you list them? Answers are on the next page. (Hint...there are four ferocious felines.)

No cheating!

125

Quiz Answers

Smiling Fish	Miami Dolphins
Woolly Bison	Buffalo Bills
Western Dudes	Dallas Cowboys
Western Steeds	Denver Broncos
Ponies	Indianapolis Colts
Ferocious Felines	Charlotte Panthers
	Cincinnati Bengals
	Detroit Lions
	Jacksonville Jaguars
Wildcatters	Houston Oilers
Pirates	Los Angeles Raiders
	Tampa Bay Buccaneers
Ursine Mammals	Chicago Bears
Norsemen	Minnesota Vikings
Indians	Kansas City Chiefs
	Washington Redskins
Miners	Pittsburgh Steelers
	San Francisco Forty-Niners
Birds	Atlanta Falcons
	Arizona Cardinals
	Philadelphia Eagles
	Seattle Seahawks
Sheep	Los Angeles Rams
Loyalists	Boston Patriots
Goliaths	New York Giants
Meat Processors	Green Bay Packers
Color	Cleveland Browns
Holy People	New Orleans Saints
Lightening Bolts	San Diego Chargers
Modern Aircraft	New York Jets

126

Football Quotables

Oh, he's football crazy,
he's football mad and
the football has robbed
him o' the wee bit of
sense he had.
Football Crazy (1960 Song)
Jimmy MacGregor

Victory shifts from man to man.
Homer

In life, as in a football game,
the principle to follow is: hit the
line hard.
Theodore Roosevelt
Ib. The American Boy

Victory has a thousand fathers,
but defeat is an orphan.
JFK

(In war)...there is no substitute
for victory...
Douglas MacArthur,
April 19, 1951

I always turn to the sports
page first. They record people's
accomplishments: the front page,
nothing but man's failure...
Earl Warren

When you win, nothing hurts...
Joe Namath

I do not think that winning is the
most important thing. I think that
winning is the only thing...
Vince Lombardi

...it is a war minus the shooting.
George Orwell
The Sporting Spirit

Some people think football is a
matter of life and death...I can
assure them it is much more
serious than that...
Bill Shankly
Scottish footballer 1914-1981

Have players wear gloves with
batteries inside, so their helmets
will light up when they get the ball,
and everybody can see who has it...
Christie Brinkley

A game that requires an ambulance
on the field at all times is not
exactly a light-hearted pursuit...
Fran Leibowitz

American football is an occasion in
which dancing girls, bands, tactical
huddles, and television commercial
breaks are interrupted by short
bursts of play.
The London Times

On training:

A pint of sweat will save
a gallon of blood...
George Patton,
November 8, 1942

127

Do You Think...

That a "quick delivery" is what every woman hopes for in her ninth month of pregnancy?

That a "chain gang" is a group of maximum security inmates?

That a "cheap shot" is the bar whiskey at a honky-tonk saloon?

That "good coverage" is found at the make-up counter and hides lines, circles, and zits?

That a "crackback" is an Oriental massage?

That "down-and-out" refers to the homeless?

That a "fair catch" is a bachelor with no ex-wives, children, or debt?

That "penetration" is the title of a X-rated movie?

That a "sack" is a baggy dress style that goes in and out of fashion?

That a "gap" is a reason for a dental appointment?

That "hashmarks" are German money?

That a "long snapper" is a prize-winning fish from the Gulf of Mexico?

That "flat" means a tiny (32AAAA) bra?

That the "coffin corner" is a shop where one can buy burial supplies?

That an "illegal chuck" is a pot roast that got by the meat inspector?

That "reverse" is a button on your VCR?

That being "caught in the grasp" is something that happens prior to marriage?

That to "turn the corner" means that one is finally getting over another one of life's humps?

That a "gridiron" is stored in your pantry and has to be heated before using?

If so, please read on...

128

Audible—A change of plays, shouted in code by the quarterback at the line of scrimmage.

Backfield—Area behind the line of scrimmage.

Backpedal—Backward running to drop into pass coverage.

Ball Control—An offensive team maintaining possession of the football by running and passing the ball.

Blindside—The side opposite from the quarterback's throwing arm where he has less than optimal vision when setting to throw.

Blitz—A pass rush involving defensive backs or linebackers.

Block—The technique with which an offensive player attacks a defensive player, hoping to knock him out of the play.

Bomb—A long pass.

Bootleg—A surprise play in which the quarterback carries the hidden ball away from the direction of the play.

Bubble Butt—Large buttocks and thigh area; considered a positive.

Bump-and-Run—A type of pass coverage in which a defensive back pushes and delays a receiver at the line of scrimmage.

Chain Gang—The men who move the sideline markers.

Cheap Shot—An unsportsmanlike illegal hit.

Clipping—An illegal block from behind.

Coffin Corner—A punt that goes out of bounds inside the ten-yard line.

Coin Toss—Team captains meet in center of the field to determine which team will kick off and which team will receive the ball. The visiting team makes the call.

Conversion—This occurs after a touchdown has been scored. The scoring team can either kick through the goalposts for one point or run or pass into the end zone for two points.

Coverage—Pass defense.

Crackback—An offensive player blocks back on a defensive player unexpectedly.

Darter—A ball carrier who has the ability to change directions without losing speed.

Daylight—An opening for the ball carrier to break through and gain yardage.

Gridiron Gab

129

BLINDSIDE

Dead Ball—A ball that can no longer be advanced.

Defense—The team without the ball and their defensive scheme; the team defending their end zone.

Dime Defense—Six defensive backs are put into the game in an obvious passing situation, instead of the normal four defensive backs and two linebackers.

Down—A play from scrimmage; the offense gets four downs numbered in sequence, first to fourth, to gain ten yards and make a new first down.

Down-and-Out—A pass receiver's route downfield with a 90-degree cut toward the sidelines.

Draft—The method by which college players are selected by the professional teams.

Encrypted—The scrambling of signals when using radio helmets to send plays onto the field. The encryption scheme contains more than 268 million possible codes.

Encroachment—A penalty that occurs when a player moves into the neutral zone making contact with an opposing player before the ball is snapped.

End Zone—The area into which the offense must move the ball to score a touchdown.

Extra Point—The one-point play allowed a team after scoring a touchdown. Also called a "conversion" or "P.A.T." (point-after-touchdown).

Face Mask—A penalty that occurs when the defender grabs the ball carrier's face mask as a means of tackling.

Fair Catch—A free catch by the receiver of a punt or kickoff signaled by receiver raising one arm. Once a receiver raises his arm he is not allowed to advance the ball and may not be tackled.

Field Goal—A scoring kick over the crossbar and between the uprights that is worth three points.

Flanker—The wide receiver on the tight end's side of the line, usually split out.

Flashes—A player shows sporadic evidence of athletic ability.

Flat—The offensive backfield area near sidelines.

131

Four-Three—A defensive formation with four defensive linemen, three linebackers, and four defensive backs.

Free Agent—A player who is job hunting.

Front—The defensive linemen.

Fumble—Losing possession of the ball.

Game Clock—Official clock which monitors the time of the game.

Game Plan—Coaching strategy prepared before a game based on the talent and tendencies of both teams.

Gap—The space between two linemen.

Goal Line—The field stripe separating the end zone from the field of play. Must be crossed or touched to score a touchdown.

Hail Mary—A desperation pass, usually at the end of a half or a game, wherein the ball is thrown, and a Prayful Hail Mary is said that someone catches it.

Halftime—A rest period between the two halves.

Hand Off—The quarterback giving the ball to another player, usually a running back.

Hang Time—The amount of time a punt or kick stays in the air after leaving the kicker's foot.

Hashmarks—Short lines running the length of the field and lined up with goal post uprights. Used for spotting the ball.

Holding—The penalty called for illegally grabbing or grasping another player.

Hole—A space created by offensive blockers on the line of scrimmage through which the ball carrier can run.

Huddle—A brief team gathering for calling plays and signals.

"I" Formation—A fullback and tailback aligned behind the center and quarterback in a straight line forming an "I."

Intentional Grounding—The quarterback intentionally throws the ball away in order to avoid being sacked. This usually results in a penalty.

Interception—A defensive player catches a pass intended for an offensive player. This changes team possession.

Interference—A judgement penalty called when an offensive or defensive player illegally prevents another player from catching a pass.

133

HANG TIME

In the Grasp—A penalty that occurs when a defender grabs the quarterback in such a way that it is considered a sack, even though the quarterback may not be thrown to the ground.

In the Tank—A term for the length of time that it takes for an injured player to return to play.

Juke—Elusive move by ball carrier to avoid a tackler.

Key—The offensive player that a defender is coached to watch in order to gain clues as to the direction of a play.

Lateral—A backward toss or pass.

Line of Scrimmage (L.O.S.)—The line on which the ball is placed and from which the play begins.

Long-Strider—A player who takes long steps, as opposed to short quick steps, and therefore tends to move slower into and out of his breaks.

Long-Snapper—The center who snaps the ball to the punter or holder on a field goal or P.A.T. (point after touchdown).

Man-to-Man—A type of defense in which linebackers and defensive backs are each assigned an individual receiver to cover (as opposed to "zone" coverage).

Man in Motion—The action of a running back or receiver, who runs behind and parallel to the line of scrimmage, before the ball is snapped.

Neutral Zone—Length of football on the line of scrimmage. No player may enter the neutral zone before the snap of the ball.

Nickel Defense—Five defensive backs are put in the game instead of the normal four.

Offense—The team who has possession of the ball.

Offsides—A penalty called when a player crosses the line of scrimmage before the ball is snapped.

Onside Kick—A short kick the kicking team hopes to recover themselves. It must go at least 10 yards.

Overtime—The extra 15-minute period played at the end of regulation game time to break a tie. Also called "sudden death" because the first team to score wins.

Pass pattern—The route the receiver runs to defeat the defensive back and catch a forward pass.

135

Penalty Marker—A yellow flag thrown by officials indicating a penalty.

Penetration—Movement of the defensive player across the line of scrimmage.

Pigskin—The oblong leather football weighing 14 to 15 oz.

Pileup—Excessive number of players tackling a ball carrier.

Placekick—The ball is held by a holder and is kicked from a fixed point.

Playbook—The book that contains the offensive and defensive schemes designed by the coaches.

Pocket—The area protected by offensive linemen in which the quarterback seeks protection while he sets up to throw the ball.

Point Spread—The number of points by which a team is favored; predicted by odds-makers; also called "the line."

Pooch—Short high punt inside the 20-yard line.

Prevent Defense—Utilized on a down in which the offensive team must throw the ball, extra defensive backs play extremely deep to stop the offense from scoring.

Red Zone—The area inside the opponent's 20-yard line where the field becomes restricted by the endline.

Roster—The list of players for each team written alphabetically or numerically.

Run and Shoot—An offense that throws the ball without a tight end in the formation.

Sack—A play in which the quarterback is tackled in the backfield while attempting to pass.

Safety—A two-point scoring play caused by tackling a ball carrier or passer in his own end zone.

Seams—The area between pass coverage zones.

Secondary—Normally four defensive backs aligned to defend the pass.

Set—The position of an offensive lineman who gets into his stance and remains motionless until the ball is snapped.

Shift—The movement of an offensive player before the ball is snapped. This changes the look of the formation.

Shotgun—The quarterback stands five to seven yards behind the center

instead of directly behind him. The center quickly snaps the ball to the quarterback who is already in a position to throw the ball.

Shuttle Pass—A short forward pitch from the quarterback to a running back in the backfield of the offensive team.

Signals—The numbers and words called by the quarterback at the line of scrimmage to put the play in motion.

Sleeper—An obscure player who starts or stars.

Slot—An area between the offensive tackle and the split end.

Snap—The action of the center passing the ball to the quarterback at the start of the play.

Spearing—A late hit by a defender in which he uses his helmet or shoulder pads to illegally hit a downed ball carrier.

Special Teams—The players who make up all phases of the kicking game; also called "suicide squads."

Spot—The placement of the ball by the referee after a play or penalty.

Squib Kick—An intentionally low kickoff that bounces about and is difficult to handle.

Stats—The statistics kept on every phase of the game and individual players.

Strong Side—The side of the offensive line with the tight end, normally the wide side of the field.

Sudden Death—An overtime period in which the team that scores first wins the game.

Suicide Squad—The players who make up special teams and cover kicks with reckless abandon.

Swingman—A player who can play more than one position.

Tailback—The deep back in the "I" formation.

Three-Four—A defensive formation with three defensive linemen, four linebackers, and four defensive backs.

Three-Point Stance—A stance used by linemen and running backs in which one hand touches the ground.

Time-Out—A halt in game action called by the referee or a team. Each team is allowed three per half.

Touchback—A non-returnable kick into the end zone which is put into play on the receiving team's 20-yard line.

Touchdown—A 6-point scoring play that occurs when a team is in possession of the ball in the opponent's end zone.

Training Camp—The site and practice time prior to the first conference game.

Turf Toe—An injury to the big toe.

Turk—The coach with the assignment of informing players that they are cut from the team.

Turning the Corner—The ability and speed of a running back to go outside and turn upfield thus outrunning the defenders.

Turnover—A change of possession that occurs when an offensive player loses the ball.

Two-Minute Warning—The official notification given to both benches that two minutes remain in the game or half.

Uncovered—Refers to a player who has no opponent lined up directly across from him.

Uprights—Two vertical poles of the goalpost between which a field goal or extra point must pass.

Wave—The fans' participation in the game by standing and waving their arms in unison in successive sections of the stands.

Weak side—The side of the offensive line without the tight end, normally the short side of the field.

Zone—A type of coverage in the defensive secondary in which the cornerbacks and safeties are assigned specific areas to defend (as opposed to "man-to-man" coverage).

141

Team Prayer

We pray our team is fired up,
our coaching staff alert!
We ask you, Lord, protect our men,
so no one will be hurt.
Help our offense take that ball,
and get it to the goal.
May we not make one mistake,
but maintain ball control.
May our receivers get downfield
in a flash of dashing speed,
and catch the passes sent their way
for all the points we need.
Let our quarterback be hot,
inspire him today.
When our men clip or jump offsides,
may refs' eyes go astray.
If their fans are praying, too,
heed not their dissertation.
Ignore them, please, attend our needs
and hear our supplication.
And when the final seconds wane,
and the clock runs out,
may we emerge victorious!
That's what it's all about!

Amen

143